Canadian Writing Series

SENTENCE WRITING
GRADES 4 TO 6

Written by Marie-Helen Goyetche

This book will help you introduce, explain and practise the different types of sentences including compound & complex sentences, declarative, exclamatory, interrogative and imperative with your students. An introduction to figures of speech including Metaphors, Similies, Personification, Onomatopoeia, and Oxymoron. Practise worksheets look at verb tenses plus writing paragraphs, main idea, topic sentence, supporting sentences and concluding sentences. Writing prompts for Narrative, Descriptive, Persuasive/Opinion and Expository writing styles are also included.

Marie-Helen Goyetche is an elementary school principal and freelance writer. Marie-Helen received her Bachelors in Education from Concordia University and her Masters in Educational Leadership from Bishops University. She has over 100 articles and over 40 curriculum books published.

Copyright © On The Mark Press 2016

This publication may be reproduced under licence from Access Copyright, or with the express written permission of On The Mark Press, or as permitted by law. All rights are otherwise reserved, and no part of this publication may be reproduced, stored in a retrieval system, or transmitted in any form or by any means, electronic, mechanical, photocopying, scanning, recording or otherwise, except as specifically authorized.

All Rights Reserved.
Printed in Canada.

Published in Canada by:
On The Mark Press
15 Dairy Avenue, Napanee, Ontario, K7R 1M4
www.onthemarkpress.com

Funded by the Government of Canada

R1154 ISBN: 978-1-4877-0441-4 © On The Mark Press

At A Glance

In this book you will find how to introduce, explain and practise:

A review of basic sentences found in Sentences Writing Grades 1 to 3.
A review of all the different types of sentences such as declarative, exclamatory, interrogative and imperative.
Answering Questions
An introduction to figures of speech such as Metaphors, Similes, Personification, Onomatopoeia and Oxymoron.
Compound & Complex Sentences
Practise worksheets
A look at verb tenses; past-tense, present-tense and future-tense
Working on writing paragraphs: main idea, topic sentence, supporting sentences and concluding sentences.
Writing Prompts for Narrative, Descriptive, Persuasive/Opinion and Expository Writing styles
Creating a Cheat Sheet
Tips on creating a Writing Centre

Table of Contents

At A Glance 2
How to use this book 4
Trait-Based Writing 5
Rubric Teacher and Student 6
Writing Centre page 7
Sentence Checklist Teacher/Peer and Self 8

Complete or Incomplete 9
Declarative Sentences 10
Yes/No Questions 11
Alternative Questions 12
WH- Questions 13
Tag Questions 14
Writing Answers 15
Exclamatory Sentences 16
Imperative Sentences 17
Subjects and Predicates 18
Verb Tenses 19

Compound & Complex Sentences 22
Run On Sentences 25

Figure of Speech 30
Metaphors 31
Similes 34
Personification 38
Alliteration 40
Assonance 41
Hyperbole 42
Figure of Speech 44
Idioms 45
Onomatopoeia 49
Oxymoron 52
Pun 54
Riddles 55
Worksheet 56
Tongue Twister 57

Colon, Semi-Colon, Comma, Dash 59

Paragraph Writing 62
Main Ideas 63
Topic Sentences 65
Supporting Sentences 69
Concluding Sentences 72
Paragraph worksheet 74
Descriptive Writing 76
Narrative Writing 78
Expository Writing 80
Persuasive/Personal Opinion 82

Answer Key 83
Cheat Sheet 85

R1154 ISBN: 978-1-4877-0441-4 © On The Mark Press

 # How to use this book

In this book you will find:

- An overview of the Trait-Based Writing.

- Writing Task Rubrics for both teacher and student use based on the Trait-Based Writing.

- A teacher/peer and student writing checklist to work on between the draft and good copy.

- A review of the basic sentence types found in Sentence Writing Grade 1 to 3 with practise pages.

- This book is fully reproducible. There are at least two ways this book can be used: make reproducible copies for all students as they are good reminders of the different types of sentences, and introduction to grammar and figure speech. The students work on their own booklet during the school year, at their own pace.

- Another way is to have teacher introduce concept to students and allow students to work on each concept as they are presented.

- If you have weaker students, the Sentence Writing Grade 1 to 3, offers, more practise sheets, a personal book containing word lists and a Sentence Creator activity.

- There are many writing prompts for the four types of writing styles Narrative, Descriptive, Persuasive/Opinion and Expository Writing styles.

- Practise sheets on writing a paragraph – step-by-step. Good for introducing and also good for review.

- Sentence writing can be fun hence, tongue twisters, riddles, puns, onomatopoeia, hyperbole, oxymoron and idioms are included in this sentence writing book.

Trait-Based Writing

Organization

- Sequencing
- Using beginning, middle and end
- Writing a complete piece
- Logical order
- Transition

Voice

- Looking at Point-of-view
- Choosing the right point-of-view for the right purpose
- Using different voices
- Using own words

Ideas

- Good knowledge of topic
- Stays on topic
- Elaborating and developing ideas on topic
- Is specific on topic

Conventions

- Writes clear sentences (no run-ons) me-
- Mechanics of writing
- Uses punctuation
- Spelling
- Grammar

Word Choice & Details

- Using action words
- Adding and using descriptive words (Adjectives and Adverbs)
- The details are staying on topic
- Using expressions the audience will understand

Sentence Fluency

- Flowing sentences
- Smooth paragraph
- Use of short and long sentences

 # WRITING Centre

If you want your students to write, you have to have them writing. Writing for a child who is not well equipped, does not understand how-to, has too many ideas and not sure how to put them down on paper will be a very frustrating. Create a Writing Centre within your classroom. It won't take you too much time to set and can use many recycled items to lure your students into creative writing. Make it fun rather than making it a chore and they will be asking you if they can write!

You will need an area or corner away from the main door.

A few tables and chairs. Foot stools are great too so they don't get distracted with dangling feet.

Use prompts and posters; i.e. transition words, connecting words, adjectives etc. and change them regularly to inspire them. Have a few dictionaries too: English, Rhyming, and Thesaurus.

On the tables, have different types of paper available for writing. Have on hand recycled paper for their rough drafts and for their good copy stationary, index cards, lined paper, coloured-paper, writing pads, envelopes, postcards, greeting cards, stickers and stamps.

A laptop/computer for publishing on the web.

Include a tray/box with writing examples such as a map, a flyer, a menu, a recipe, a craft, a poem etc.

Include a tray/box where the students can put their drafts when they feel it is ready for editing.

Include a tray/box of various worksheets such as those found in this book to allow children to practise, refresh and learn at their own pace.

Allow each student to have access to the Sentence Creator in this book. Let them take their imagination and write, write and write!

Make a big deal of published pieces. Create a Reading corner with lots of their stories. Upload them to the school web sites. Have a monthly Author's Tea to celebrate the wonderful writing your students write. If you make a big deal of it – they will reward you with interest and many, many stories!

Teacher Rubric Evaluation: Writing Tasks

Name of Student: _____   Title: _____

	1	2	3	4
Beginning Middle End (Organization)	The sentences are not in any order	There is some attempt at Beginning/Middle/End	Beginning/Middle/End are all present	Interesting and complete Beginning/Middle/End
Ideas	The main idea is not clear	The idea needs to be worked on	There is one main idea	There is one main idea and sub (ideas)
Details	Details need to be added	More details are needed	You have many details	You have many excellent details
Word Choice	The same words are used over and over again	You use one or two new words	You used many new words and expressions	Excellent vocabulary
Sentence Fluency	The piece does not make sense	The piece is somewhat clear	The piece is clear	The piece is clear, and the audience is targeted
Voice	The piece does not have a voice	The piece has somewhat a voice	The voice matches the purpose of the text	Point of view is clear and maintained
Conventions	Too many spelling & grammatical errors, text doesn't make sense	There are some spelling and grammatical errors	There are few spelling and grammatical errors	Spelling, grammar and mechanics of writing are clear
Creativity	No creativity is shown in the piece	There is an attempt made to be creative	There is some creativity and originality	Very creative and original

Student Self-Evaluation Rubric Evaluation: Writing Tasks

Name of Student: _____   Title: _____

	1	2	3	4
Beginning Middle End (Organization)	My sentences are not in any order	I have made an attempt to include a Beginning/Middle/End	I wrote a clear Beginning/Middle/End	I wrote an interesting and complete Beginning/Middle/End
Ideas	What is my main idea?	My idea needs to be worked on	I have one main idea	I have one main idea and some sub (ideas)
Details	I don't have any details	I need to add more details	I have many details	I have many excellent details
Word Choice	I use the same words over and over again	I added one or two new words	I added many new words and expressions	I added difficult and well-chosen words
Clearness	My work does not make sense	My work is somewhat clear	My work is clear	My work is clear, and I know who my audience is
Voice	My piece does not have a voice	My piece has somewhat a voice	My voice matches the purpose of the text	My point of view is clear and maintained
Conventions	Too many spelling & grammatical errors, my text doesn't make sense	There are some spelling and grammatical errors	There are few spelling and grammatical errors	Spelling, grammar and mechanics of writing are clear
Creativity	I do not show creativity	I have made an attempt to show creativity	I have shown some creativity and originality	I have clearly shown creativity and originality

R1154 ISBN: 978-1-4877-0441-4 © On The Mark Press

Teacher/Peer Sentence Writing Checklist

Name of Student: _____   Title: _____

Feedback by: _____

1.	There is a capital at the beginning of each sentence.	
2.	There is a punctuation mark at the end of each sentence.	
3.	There is a subject and predicate in each sentence.	
4.	The idea is present and clear in each sentence.	
5.	The message is clear.	
6.	The writing category is clear.	
7.	The sentence is written with finger spaces between each word.	
8.	There are new and some difficult words used.	
9.	There is no repetition.	
10.	There are adjectives and adverbs present.	
11.	The sentence flows well when read aloud.	
12.	The good copy is ready to be written.	

Student Writing Checklist

Title: _____   Written by: _____

1.	I have used a capital at the beginning of each sentence.	
2.	I have used a period, a question mark or an exclamation mark.	
3.	I included a subject and a predicate in my sentence.	
4.	My idea is present and clear.	
5.	My message is clear.	
6.	The writing category is clear.	
7.	My sentence is clear and has a finger space between words on the written page.	
8.	I have used new and some difficult words.	
9.	I don't repeat.	
10.	I have used adjectives and adverbs.	
11.	My sentence flows well when I read it aloud.	
12.	I am ready to now do my good copy.	

R1154 ISBN: 978-1-4877-0441-4 © On The Mark Press

COMPLETE OR INCOMPLETE

A complete sentence expresses a complete thought to the reader.

- I always wear my blue running shoes for gym class. **(A Sentence)**
- Blue running shoes for gym class. **(Not a sentence)**

Put a check mark on the line at the end of each complete sentence or an X if the sentence is incomplete.

1. Billy went to the store to buy a chocolate bar. _____
2. Ran away fast. _____
3. The King rode his horse through the village and waved to the villagers. _____
4. The car stopped. _____
5. Veronica walked around. _____
6. The cat scratched the couch with her sharp claws. _____
7. A new recipe in the book. _____
8. She finished reading Harry Potter in only 3 days. _____
9. There are 7 books. _____
10. It was a gray and stormy day so we stayed inside and watched a movie. _____

Do you remember writing questions? _____

Read the questions below. Make a check mark next to the sentence if the question is correct and an X if it is not.

1. Do you want a hotdog or a hamburger? _____
2. Aren't you the one, aren't you? _____
3. Have you been here before? _____
4. The bus left already? _____
5. Who remembers how to write sentences correctly? _____

Share and compare your answers with a fellow classmate.

DECLARATIVE SENTENCES

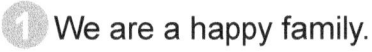

A Declarative Sentence gives us information. A Declarative Sentence starts with a capital letter, the sentences tells us something and the sentence ends in a period (.).

Here are some examples of Declarative Sentences:

1. We are a happy family.
2. The shopping bag is red.
3. The stars are bright.
4. The mechanic fixes cars.
5. The tire is flat.

Now write ten declarative sentences of your own below.

1. _____
2. _____
3. _____
4. _____
5. _____
6. _____
7. _____
8. _____
9. _____
10. _____

INTERROGATIVE SENTENCES

There are four types of questions. You will use different types of questions depending on what type of information you are looking for. An Interrogative Sentence asks for information. Each interrogative sentence will start with a Capital letter, the words will ask for information and will end with a question mark (?)

Here are some examples of Yes/No Interrogative Sentences, with complete answers

1. Do you like music?   Yes, I like music.
2. Have you done your homework?   No, I have not done my homework.
3. Do you have a hobby?   Yes, I crochet.
4. Do you like potato chips?   Yes, I like potato chips.
5. Did you go shopping?   No, I do not like shopping.

Now write eight Yes/No Interrogative Sentences below.
Have a fellow student answer the questions.

1. _____
2. _____
3. _____
4. _____
5. _____
6. _____
7. _____
8. _____

INTERROGATIVE SENTENCES

There are four types of questions. You will use different types of questions depending on the type of information that you are looking for. The second type is called Alternative Questions. In your questions you are providing choices and the person answering your question can pick one of the answers. Practise writing and answering Alternative Questions using the spaces below.

1. Do you want toast or oatmeal?   The answer you are predicting to hear will be either:
   I would like toast please. OR I would like oatmeal please.

2. Do you want to go to eat now or later? _____

3. Do you want to watch a movie or a TV show? _____

4. Did you see a movie, a show or a play? _____

5. Did you visit your old school or your old house? _____

6. Did you want pizza with pepperoni and cheese or just cheese? _____

7. _____ ? _____

8. _____ ? _____

9. _____ ? _____

10. _____ ? _____

Compare your questions and answers with a partner.
Draw a picture to explain one of your sentences.

INTERROGATIVE SENTENCES

There are four types of questions. You will use different types of questions depending on the type of information that you are looking for. The third type is called WH Questions. You are asking questions where the information asks the 7 WH Questions. Who? What? When? Where? Why? Which? And How? Provide two choices and the person answering your question can pick one or the other.

Practise writing and answering WH Questions using the spaces below

1. Who would like a tennis racquet?   The answer you are predicting to hear could be: I would like a tennis racquet.

2. What make of tennis racquet would you like?
_____

3. When would you like your tennis racquet?
_____

4. Where do you want to use your tennis racquet?
_____

5. Why did you choose a tennis racquet?
_____

6. Which sport is your favourite sport?
_____

7. How do you play tennis?
_____

Now choose a topic you like: _____

1. Who _____?

2. What _____?

3. When _____?

4. Where _____?

5. Why _____?

6. Which _____?

7. How _____?

Share and compare answers with a partner.

 R1154 ISBN: 978-1-4877-0441-4 © On The Mark Press

WRITING ANSWERS

Writing good answers is just as important as writing good questions. Good answers include: a capital letter, the sentence stands alone and ends with the correct punctuation mark.

1. Do you want some fruit? _____

2. Do you like the birthday cake? _____

3. Do you know Mrs. Smith? _____

4. Would you like ham, tuna or roast beef on your sandwich?
   _____

5. Would you like marshmallow, sprinkles or nuts on your ice cream?
   _____

6. Will you be going flying or driving this summer? _____

7. Who played with the cards? _____

8. Where did they play tennis? _____

9. Which day did they go? _____

10. You play piano, don't you? _____

11. You got the book, didn't you? _____

12. You will go to see her, won't you? _____

Now write some questions and answers of your own.

13. _____? _____

14. _____? _____

15. _____? _____

16. _____? _____

17. _____? _____

14   R1154 ISBN: 978-1-4877-0441-4 © On The Mark Press

EXCLAMATORY SENTENCES

An Exclamatory Sentence not only tells information but it expresses emotions. It is also used when you use interjections. You will see an exclamatory sentence when the sentence starts with a capital – expresses emotion or a feeling and ends with an exclamation mark.

Here are some examples of Exclamatory Sentences:

1. Aww!
2. Oh!
3. Rats!
4. Darn!
5. Eeeewww!

Now write your own interjections or exclamatory sentences.

6. _____
7. _____
8. _____
9. _____
10. _____
11. _____
12. _____
13. _____
14. _____
15. _____

IMPERATIVE SENTENCES

An Imperative Sentence is also known as a command or a request that absolutely has to be done. The sentence starts with a capital letter, gives a command or request and may finish with a period (.) or an exclamation mark (!).

Here are some examples of Imperative Sentences:

1. Look!
2. Make your bed.
3. Drink your milk.
4. Eat your broccoli!
5. Go!

Now write your own imperative sentences.

1. _____
2. _____
3. _____
4. _____
5. _____
6. _____
7. _____
8. _____
9. _____
10. _____

SUBJECT & PREDICATE

The subject in a sentence answers who or what the sentence is about. The predicate is the rest of the sentence that describes the subject.

For example: The girl looked at herself in the mirror.

Read each sentence below. Underline the subject and circle the predicate.

1. Mattia typed on the computer keyboard.
2. The French teacher wrote the instructions on the board.
3. The wool beanie kept my ears warm during the storm.
4. My favourite book was on sale at the book store.
5. The energetic children ran all over the school.
6. The lady with the running shoes taught Zumba.
7. George and John walked to the gym after school.
8. The enthusiastic fans cheered when the hockey player scored.
9. The tired principal got into her car at the end of the day.
10. Ms. Sarah's students went on a field trip to the space centre.
11. We met the boys at the movie theatre.
12. My best friend Liane moved to a city six hours away.

Now write your own complete sentences with subjects and predicates.

13. _____
14. _____
15. _____
16. _____
17. _____
18. _____
19. _____
20. _____

Share and compare your sentences with a partner.

SUBJECT & PREDICATE

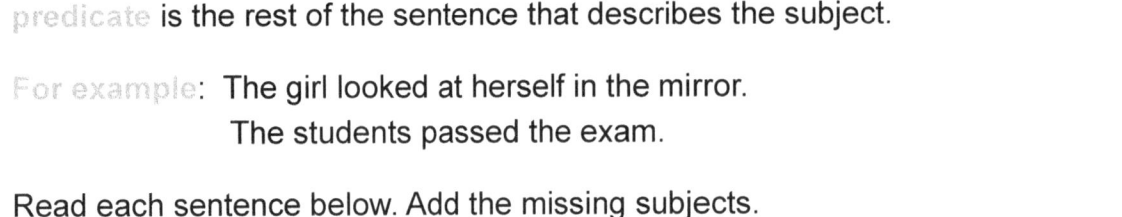

The subject in a sentence answers who or what the sentence is about. The predicate is the rest of the sentence that describes the subject.

For example: The girl looked at herself in the mirror.
             The students passed the exam.

Read each sentence below. Add the missing subjects.

Example: _____ heard a loud noise.   Answer: The man heard a loud noise.

1. _____ walked to the assembly.
2. _____ spoke to the students.
3. _____ went to class in the morning.
4. _____ was sad for her students.
5. _____ were relieved that they won the game.
6. _____ won the race.
7. _____ made lunch.
8. _____ cheered loudly.
9. _____ was lost in the crowd.
10. _____ hit a homerun.
11. _____ went shopping at the mall.
12. _____ scored a goal.

Now read each sentence below and fill in the predicate to each sentence below.

Example: The boys_____.   Answer: The boys played soccer.

1. Susan _____.
2. The girls _____.
3. The dog _____.
4. The class _____.
5. The students _____.
6. The car _____.
7. The kittens _____.
8. The puppies _____.
9. The boys _____.
10. The spectators _____.
11. The employees_____.
12. The bees_____.

18   R1154 ISBN: 978-1-4877-0441-4 © On The Mark Press

VERB TENSES

The Past-Tense of a verb tells us the action has already happened.
The Present-Tense of a verb tells us the action is happening now.
The future-Tense of a verb tells us the action will happen in the future.

Read the verbs below, write the verb in the correct tense.

Verb	Past	Present	Future
Example: hop	hopped	is hopping	will hop
1 run			
2 jump			
3 skip			
4 laugh			
5 leap			
6 shoot			
7 dribble			
8 pass			
9 sit			
10 sprint			
11 block			
12 eat			
13 write			
14 sleep			
15 walk			

VERB TENSES

The Past-Tense of a verb tells us the action has already happened.
The Present-Tense of a verb tells us the action is happening now.
The Future-Tense of a verb tells us the action will happen in the future.

Read the sentences below, identify the verb tense and then change the tense of the verb and re-write the new sentence. You may choose the new verb-tense.

Example: Dan went to school. Past-Tense

Dan will be going to school. Future-Tense

1. Brian takes the bus to school. _____

2. The choir left the stage. _____

3. The moon is shining bright. _____

4. There are many items in the basket. _____

5. The kids will be going on a fieldtrip. _____

6. I love that TV show. _____

7. The patient coughed and coughed and coughed. _____

8. The doctor was late for his appointment. _____

9. The computer will be coming next week. _____

10. The bicycle is red. _____

IRREGULAR VERBS

The Past-Tense of a verb tells us the action has already happened but not all Past-Tense verbs will end with – ed.

Read the sentences below, circle the right verb that will complete the sentence.

1. Vanessa _____ a solo during the concert. (sing   sang   singed)

2. Niko and Gabriel _____ happy to see us. (were   is   are)

3. My grandmother _____ to visit Mexico last year. (went   go   will)

4. Frank _____ the chick pox last month. (has   had   will have)

5. Mom _____ the book with us. (read   red   is reading)

6. The boss _____ the employees. (pay   paid   payed)

7. I _____ the truth. (tell   told   will tell)

8. You _____ the answer. (know   knew   knowed)

9. We _____ in line for an hour. (stand   stood   standed)

10. The cell-phone _____. (ring   rang   rung)

11. John _____ to take his vitamin. (forget   forgot   forgotten)

12. Dan and Helen _____ the lemonade. (drinked   drank   drunk)

13. The vegetables _____ well in the garden. (grow   grew   grown)

14. The water on the pond _____. (freeze   froze   frozen)

15. The kindergarten child _____ his mittens. (loose   lose   lost)

16. We _____ under the bed while Julie looked for us. (hide   hid   hidden)

17. The snake _____ my ankle. (bit   bite   bait)

18. Mr. Jones _____ the principal. (became   become   began)

19. Billy _____ the joke and laughed. (get   gut   got)

20. The day _____ with a bright, warm sun. (begun   began   begin)

COMPOUND SENTENCES

A compound sentence is when you join two main clauses together with a connective like a comma or conjunction.

EXAMPLES: I like to dance and I like to sing.
Joey can be loud at times but he is a quiet boy.

You can make compound sentences by combining two simple sentences together with a comma or a conjunction. Create as many compound sentences as you can using the list of simple sentences and conjunctions below.

SIMPLE SENTENCES	CONJUNCTIONS
A squirrel sat on a tree branch.	so
I was painting a picture.	but
It was cold and windy outside.	and
A puppy followed me home from school.	or
I gave it a bone.	,
My sister had a map of the forest.	
We got lost in the trees.	

1. _____
2. _____
3. _____
4. _____
5. _____
6. _____
7. _____
8. _____

COMPOUND SENTENCES

A compound sentence is when you join two main clauses together with a connective like a comma or a semi colon.

A semicolon is used to join independent clauses that are lengthy and already joined with a comma.

EXAMPLE
Independent Clause   John made cookies. Joe brought the milk.
Compound Sentence 1   John made cookies, and Joe brought the milk.
Compound Sentence 2   John made cookies; Joe brought the milk.

Re-write each sentence and make the necessary corrections.

1. We couldn't go play outside.
   It was very cold and snowing. (so)
   _____

2. I wanted to play on the computer.
   Mom made me do my homework.
   _____

3. The pigs rolled around in the mud.
   They did not care that they were getting dirty. (;)
   _____

4. We put our towels on the clothesline
   The sun dried them quickly (;)
   _____

5. Would you like to play Lego?
   Would you like to play checkers? (or)
   _____

COMPLEX SENTENCES

A complex sentence has an independent clause and a dependent clause. An independent clause is a complete sentence that can stand on its own and no information is left unanswered. A dependent clause is not a complete sentence because it can't stand on its own and it most likely starts with so, because or since.

Read each sentence below. Write a dependent clause to complete each complex sentence using the conjunctions so, because or since.

Example The boy is mad.
The boy is mad, because he had extra homework.

1. The students went on a field-trip _____

2. The girl received a text message _____

3. My mother sent me to the store _____

4. Dad was angry _____

5. I enjoy crafting _____

6. My favourite game is Monopoly _____

7. I have been a good student _____

8. My friends are great _____

Read the sentences below, now write an independent clause to compete the sentences.

1. _____ so he would be there on time.
2. _____ because he was grumpy.
3. _____ because he was hurt.
4. _____ since I have been a little girl.
5. _____ because he was going to be late.
6. _____ because he is the best.
7. _____ since I last spoke to you.
8. _____ so he thinks.

24   R1154 ISBN: 978-1-4877-0441-4 © On The Mark Press

RUN-ON SENTENCES

A run on sentence is two independent sentences that have been joined together in the wrong way either with the wrong punctuation or no punctuation at all.

Here are examples: I gave Mike my t-shirt, it was too big for me. = Run-on Sentence
I gave Mike my t-shirt. It was too big for me. = Correct sentences

Read the following sentences. Re-write the sentences to make two complete sentences instead.

1. The cat went up the tree and couldn't get down I called the fire department to help me get it down.

_____
_____

2. I wanted to keep the cat Dad said I wasn't allowed.

_____
_____

3. Mom made me put signs up to try and find the cat's owner I really wanted to keep the cat.

_____
_____

4. A nice old lady called mom, she thanked her for finding her cat.

_____
_____

5. I was very sad when the old lady came to pick up her cat I was happy that we helped find the cat's home even though I wanted to keep it.

_____
_____

6. The cat was very hungry, it kept crying and crying and crying.

_____
_____

7. I was very sad when the old lady came to pick up her cat, I was happy that we helped find the cat's home even though I wanted to keep it.

_____
_____

RUN-ON SENTENCES

A run-on sentence is two independent sentences that have been joined together in the wrong way either with the wrong punctuation or no punctuation at all.

Here are examples: I gave Mike my t-shirt, it was too big for me. = Run-on Sentence
I gave Mike my t-shirt. It was too big for me. = Correct sentences

Read the following sentences. Re-write the sentences to make two complete sentences instead.

1. The girl talked on the phone I waited for her to get off.
_____
_____

2. Don't run around the pool it's too dangerous.
_____
_____

3. She skipped to the park danced to the yard.
_____
_____

4. I sent a package it never arrived.
_____
_____

5. The kids in the pool splashed a lot of water it hurt my eyes.
_____
_____

6. Sun shone on the flowers in the garden.
_____
_____

7. It is important to ask questions don't you agree.
_____
_____

RUN-ON SENTENCES

A run on sentence is two independent sentences that have been joined together in the wrong way either with the wrong punctuation or no punctuation at all.

Here are examples: I gave Mike my t-shirt, it was too big for me. = Run-on Sentence
I gave Mike my t-shirt. It was too big for me. = Correct sentences

Read the following sentences. Re-write the sentences to make two complete sentences instead.

1. Our hockey game finished early we went to watch Jessie's.
_____
_____

2. We went swimming we had the day off.
_____
_____

3. I was listening to music it wasn't loud enough.
_____
_____

4. The lunch line was long we had to wait for 20 minutes.
_____
_____

5. Rosa said we shouldn't go I think so.
_____
_____

6. He made me laugh the joke was funny.
_____
_____

7. My skateboard is broken his works much better.
_____
_____

 R1154 ISBN: 978-1-4877-0441-4 © On The Mark Press

RUN-ON SENTENCES

A run-on sentence is two independent sentences that have been joined together in the wrong way either with the wrong punctuation or no punctuation at all.

Here are examples: I gave Mike my t-shirt, it was too big for me. = Run-on Sentence
I gave Mike my t-shirt. It was too big for me. = Correct sentences

Read the following sentences. Re-write the sentences to make two complete sentences instead.

1. The house next door had a fire they had no insurance.
_____
_____

2. We worked from morning till night to pick up the leaves outside it was fall.
_____
_____

3. I was looking down the street the only thing I could hear was the horn.
_____
_____

4. The town was beside the river the mountain was on the other side.
_____
_____

5. Everyone had a great time at the picnic Bob couldn't go he was working.
_____
_____

6. He broke the glass the glass was too slippery.
_____
_____

7. My friend sat at the edge of the pool the water was too cold.
_____
_____

LITERAL & FIGURATIVE LANGUAGE

Literal Language: The writing is exactly as seen. For example: The milk is white. The chocolate is brown. There is no question or underlying meaning.

Figurative Language: The writing is used to create a special effect.

You wouldn't use each type of figurative language within the same text. Using it sparsely and at the right time will make readers wanting more of your writing. Too much Figurative Language will turn off your readers. Below you will find the different types of Figurative Language. Many of them can be used in poetry.

Alliteration: Alliteration is a literary device in which many words in the sentence have the same consonant sound

Examples:
Peter Piper picked a picked a peck of pickled peppers.
Lazy leaping lizards like licking lollipops.
Kind kangaroo kick kool kites

Hyperbole: A Hyperbole is an exaggerated statement.

Example:
My backpack weighs a ton.
I can write a million examples of hyperboles.

Idiom: An idiom is an expression that doesn't exactly mean what the words say.

Example:
She has another card up her sleeve.
She spilled the beans.

Metaphor: A metaphor is a word or phrase that is used to make a comparison between two people, things, animals, or places that are not the same.

Example:
Dan is a sly fox. David is green with envy. My day was a train wreck.

Onomatopoeia: Onomatopoeia is a word that actually imitate the sound as it is happening.

Example:
Slam! Slush!
Boom! POW!

Personification: Personification is giving human characteristics and/or qualities to nonhuman objects. The characteristics could be emotions, desire or speech.

Example: The statue smiled at the crowd.

Simile: Similes are a way of comparing two things using the words like or as.

Example:
She sang like the morning dove. Her voice was as clear as glass.

FIGURES OF SPEECH

Read the sentences below. Can you identify which figure of speech is used?

ALLITERATION   HYPERBOLE   METAPHOR   PERSONIFICATION   SIMILES

1. Brad wore his black and blue blazer. _____
2. I am so hungry I can eat a horse. _____
3. The wool blanket was fluffy like cotton candy. _____
4. You are my guardian angel. _____
5. "Please Mr. Snow, keep falling so that we can have a snow-day!" _____
6. I am so tired I could sleep for a month. _____
7. Six swans went swimming in the sea. _____
8. Jump like jolly jelly jujubes. _____
9. He crept around as quiet as a mouse. _____
10. My dad can lift over two tons. _____
11. He was as angry as a grizzly bear. _____
12. The kids in school are all brains. _____
13. Gina works like a dog. _____
14. My toaster loves my toast. _____
15. My dad is my rock. _____

Now write your own definition for each figure of speech above.

ALLITERATION _____

HYPERBOLE _____

METAPHOR _____

PERSONIFICATION _____

SIMILES _____

METAPHORS

A metaphor is a word or phrase that is used to make a comparison between two people, things, animals, or places that are not the same.

For example: Dan is a sly fox. David is green with envy. My day was a train wreck.

The sentences below use metaphors. Explain the metaphor in your own words.

1. The computer in the classroom was an old dinosaur.
   _____
   _____

2. Laughter is the music of the soul.
   _____
   _____

3. Our life is a dream come true.
   _____
   _____

4. Her beautiful long and golden hair is an ocean of waves.
   _____
   _____

5. A book is the key that unlocks your imagination.
   _____
   _____

6. The teeth of a dragon are little knives.
   _____
   _____

7. Time is money.
   _____
   _____

METAPHORS

A metaphor is a word or phrase that is used to make a comparison between two people, things, animals, or places that are not the same.

For example: Dan is a sly fox. David is green with envy. My day was a train wreck.

Use the short line to write a new metaphor. Once complete, switch papers with a fellow classmate and have him/her explain your metaphors.

1. Love is _____
   _____
   _____

2. Beauty is_____
   _____
   _____

3. Courage is_____
   _____
   _____

4. Peace is_____
   _____
   _____

5. School is _____
   _____
   _____

6. Fear is_____
   _____
   _____

7. Winter is _____
   _____
   _____

METAPHORS

A metaphor is a word or phrase that is used to make a comparison between two people, things, animals, or places that are not the same.

For example: Dan is a sly fox. David is green with envy.
My day was a train wreck.

Pick two of your favourite metaphors. Write and illustrate them below.

SIMILES

Similes are a way of comparing two things using the words 'like' or 'as'.

Complete the similes below:

Like Similes = noun + verb + like + noun

1. This sun was shining like _____.

2. She sang like _____.

3. The wind whistled like _____.

4. He ran like _____.

5. The dog barks like _____.

6. The pizza smells like _____.

7. The dinner tasted like _____.

8. The trailer looked like _____.

9. She sounds like _____.

10. The book reads like _____.

Now write your own similes.

1. _____

2. _____

3. _____

4. _____

5. _____

SIMILIES

Similies are a way of comparing two things using the words 'like' or 'as'.

Complete the similies below:

Like Similes = as + adjective + as + noun

1. This leaf was as red as _____.

2. The mountain was as tall as _____.

3. It was as cold as _____.

4. She walked as slow as _____.

5. The dog barked as loud as _____.

6. The house is as dirty as _____.

7. The sister is as funny as _____.

8. The trailer is as crooked as _____.

9. Jordan is as stubborn as _____.

10. Angelina is as sweet as _____.

Now write your own like similes.

1. _____

2. _____

3. _____

4. _____

5. _____

SIMILES

Using the adjectives in the box, write 'like' or 'as' similes below.

quick	cold	beautiful	happy
thick	hot	sharp	sad
slow	tall	bright	short
energetic	funny	hungry	purple

Now write your own 'like' or 'as' similes.

1. _____

2. _____

3. _____

4. _____

5. _____

6. _____

7. _____

8. _____

9. _____

10. _____

SIMILES OR METAPHORS?

A metaphor is a word or phrase that is used to make a comparison between two people, things, animals, or places that are not the same.

A simile is a way of comparing two things using the words like or as.
Read the sentences below. Circle both subjects and write on the line if they are a metaphor or a simile.

1. This boat was as dry as the beach. _____.

2. The toy was as small as a flea. _____.

3. It rained like a shower. _____.

4. She walked as slow as molasses. _____.

5. The girl was very bright. _____.

6. The baby is an angel. _____.

7. My brother is a giant. _____.

8. The TV is as huge as a chest. _____.

9. Noah is as cute as a button. _____.

10. He read like a professional. _____.

11. She is as smart as a fox. _____.

12. The soccer ball is as hard as a rock. _____.

13. He is as quick as lightning. _____.

15. Please don't cry like a baby. _____.

PERSONIFICATION

Personification is giving human characteristics and/or qualities to nonhuman objects.

For example   The leaves danced across the schoolyard.

Draw a picture of a chosen object.

Write a list of words that describe your object's personality (human characteristics and/or qualities)

a. _____   f. _____

b. _____   g. _____

c. _____   h. _____

d. _____   I. _____

e. _____   j. _____

Write two sentences about your object.

a. _____

b. _____

PERSONIFICATION

Personification is giving human characteristics and/or qualities to nonhuman objects. The characteristics could be emotions, desire or speech.

For example: The statue smiled at the crowd.

Read the sentences below and explain the meaning and use of the personification example.

Example: The candle danced in the evening.
Meaning: The flames looked like they were swaying in the dark.

1. The heavy rain pounded the shelter.
___

2. The wheat stalks nodded in the wind.
___

3. The car happily squealed down the highway.
___

4. The smells of hot pizza pulled me into the kitchen.
___

5. It was time to wake up but the alarm clock refused to buzz.
___

6. The garden begged for water.
___

7. The mop danced across the floor.
___

8. The elephant bathed in the stream.
___

9. The lady knitted like a machine.
___

10. The leaves blew all over the yard.
___

ALLITERATION

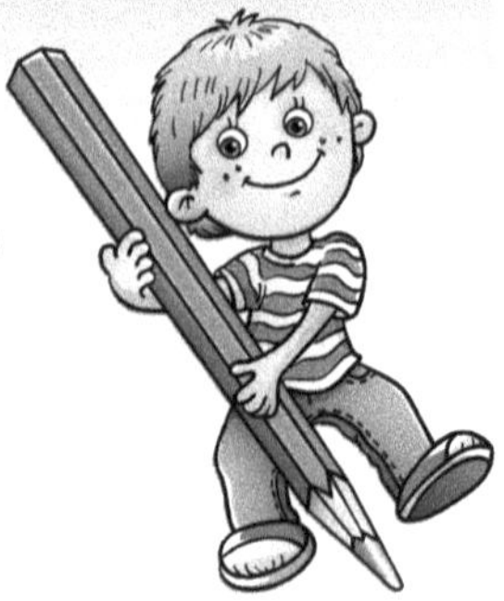

Alliteration is a literary device in which many words in the sentence have the same consonant sound.

Examples: Peter Piper picked a picked a peck of pickled peppers.

Lazy leaping lizards like licking lollipops.

Kind kangaroo kick kool kites.

Use the letters below to create your own alliterations.

B   D   G   M   N   P   R   S   T   V

1. _____

2. _____

3. _____

4. _____

5. _____

6. _____

7. _____

8. _____

9. _____

10. _____

ALLITERATION AND ASSONANCE

Alliteration is a literary device in which many words in the sentence have the same consonant sound.

Example: She sells sea shells by the sea shore.

Assonance is a literary device in which many words in the sentence have the same vowel sounds.

Example: Anna's nana asked for bananas.

Read the sentence below and write if the sentence is Alliteration or Assonance.

1. Will windy Wendy wait for wonderful Willy? _____
2. Everyone excitedly exclaimed for Emily. _____
3. Never neglect national news. _____
4. Bellowing yellow yaks chew on yucky elbows. _____
5. Tylor takes tulips to Theresa. _____
6. Patricia ate a perfect piece of pumpkin pie. _____
7. Pick a partner to practise passing. _____
8. Burt bit the bottom of the brussel sprout. _____
9. I imagine sitting proud on a round cloud. _____
10. Fleet feet sweep by sleeping sheep's. _____

Now write four sentences with assonance.

1. _____

2. _____

3. _____

4. _____

HYPERBOLE

A hyperbole is an exaggerated statement.

Example: My backpack weighs a ton.

I can write a million examples of hyperboles.

Write your own hyperboles.

1. _____

2. _____

3. _____

4. _____

5. _____

6. _____

7. _____

8. _____

9. _____

10. _____

HYPERBOLE

A hyperbole is an exaggerated statement.

Example: The whole world was staring at me.

I am so thirsty I could drink a gallon of water.

Pick two of your favourite hyperboles from the previous exercise and illustrate them below.

FIGURES OF SPEECH

Read the sentences below. Can you identify which figure of speech is used?

IDIOM   ONOMATOPOEIA   OXYMORON   PUN   UNDERSTATEMENT

1. BOOM! _____
2. I am all ears. _____
3. She was having a minor crisis. _____
4. Our base was under a tack. _____
5. It's no big deal, my cat just died. _____
6. This is your only choice. _____
7. I will have the same difference. _____
8. I have cold feet. _____
9. A little birdie told me. _____
10. POW! _____
11. I am so board. _____
12. CRUNCH! _____
13. It costs an arm and a leg. _____
14. I will have the jumbo shrimp. _____
15. Your leg is broken so it will be sore for a while. _____

Now write your own definition for each figure of speech above.

ONOMATOPOEIA _____

IDIOM _____

OXYMORON _____

PUN _____

UNDERSTATEMENT _____

44   R1154 ISBN: 978-1-4877-0441-4 © On The Mark Press

IDIOMS

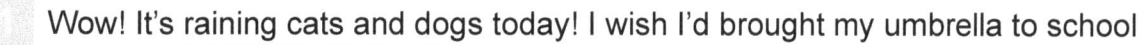

An idiom is an expression that doesn't exactly mean what the words say.

Example She has another card up her sleeve.

She spilled the beans.

Now read the sentences and try to guess the meaning of the underlined idiom.

1. Wow! It's raining cats and dogs today! I wish I'd brought my umbrella to school.
   a. I forgot my umbrella today.
   b. It's raining heavily.
   c. Cats and dogs are falling from the sky.

2. When I told my mom I would be home after midnight, she had a cow.
   a. My mom bought a baby cow.
   b. My mom is really strange.
   c. My mom was really upset.

3. It's your birthday today, a little birdie told me.
   a. I borrowed a calendar.
   b. Someone told me it was your birthday.
   c. I took a guess.

4. My brother didn't go on the roller coaster because he is a scaredy cat.
   a. My brother has a cat.
   b. My brother is a cat.
   c. My brother is afraid like a cat.

5. When the man on the phone told me I had won a trip but I had to give him my credit card number. It was a little fishy to me.
   a. I thought he smelled like a fish.
   b. I felt he was dishonest and I became suspicious of him.
   c. I thought he was playing a joke.

6. I didn't get the job, it's a dog-eat-dog world.
   a. Only the best get jobs.
   b. Dogs are allowed at the office.
   c. People treat each other like dogs.

 R1154 ISBN: 978-1-4877-0441-4 © On The Mark Press

IDIOMS

Match each sentence with the correct idiom. Write your answers below.

1. _____ 2. _____ 3. _____
4. _____ 5. _____ 6. _____

1. Sam's brother is afraid of the roller coaster.	a. It's a dog-eat-dog world.
2. It is raining heavily.	b. He's a scaredy-cat.
3. I thought the salesman was dishonest, I was suspicious.	c. It's raining cats and dogs.
4. Only the best will survive.	d. He seemed a little fishy to me.
5. An unnamed person told me.	e. She had a cow.
6. My mom was really upset when I came home late.	f. A little birdie told her.

Now re-write the sentences below using the right idioms.

1. A man tried to sell me a radio for a very, very low price. I thought that he might be a crook.

_____

2. My sister got really upset at me when I borrowed her sweater without asking her first.

_____

3. It is pouring rain out there today.

_____

4. He didn't keep up on the new information so he lost his job.

_____

5. My friends knew it was my birthday but I didn't tell them.

_____

6. Jason is very afraid of snakes.

_____

46   R1154 ISBN: 978-1-4877-0441-4 © On The Mark Press

IDIOMS

An idiom is an expression that doesn't exactly mean what the words say.

Example: She has another card up her sleeve.

      She spilled the beans.

Now read the sentences and try to guess the meaning of the underlined idiom.

1. My uncle is going out with Kelly now.

    a. They are leaving now.
    b. Kelly is leaving now.
    c. They are in a relationship now.

2. Sometimes my younger brother can drive me up the wall.

    a. I am happy with him.
    b. My brother is a terrible driver.
    c. My younger brother makes me angry.

3. I think my sister is upset with me, she is giving me the cold shoulder.

    a. My sister's shoulder is hurting her.
    b. My sister's shoulder is cold.
    c. My sister is upset with me and is ignoring me.

4. The thief was caught red-handed.

    a. The thief had red paint on his hands.
    b. The thief was caught stealing the merchandise.
    c. The thief escaped with the red merchandise.

5. When I spoke to my cousin, I gave her an earful.

    a. I gave her a present.
    b. I scolded her.
    c. She filled her ear with hot water.

6. I haven't heard anything from Janice in over a month.

    a. Janice writes.
    b. Janice can't hear.
    c. Janice hasn't communicated with anyone in over a month.

IDIOMS

Match each sentence with the correct idiom. Write your answers below.

1. _____ 2. _____ 3. _____ 4. _____
5. _____ 6. _____ 7. _____ 8. _____

1	The thief was stealing when he got caught.	a. They haven't heard from her lately.
2	My younger brother makes me angry.	b. He was caught red-handed.
3	Jennifer hasn't written or called in a very long time.	c. They are going out with each other.
4	Please contact Marie.	d. He drives me up the wall.
5	John and Susan are not dating each other anymore.	e. She's giving me the cold shoulder.
6	My mother scolded me.	f. Please get in touch with her.
7	My sister isn't speaking to me because she is angry with me.	g. She gave me an earful.
8	My uncle is in a relationship with Kelly.	h. They broke up with each other.

Now re-write the sentences below using the right idioms.

1. Mariska saw the boy take the candy from the store.

_____

2. Jason's sister was angry at him, so she yelled.

_____

3. Sally refused to talk to me, but I don't know why.

_____

4. Sometimes I get very frustrated with Jack!

_____

5. Jerry and Elaine are dating each other.

_____

48 R1154 ISBN: 978-1-4877-0441-4 © On The Mark Press

ONOMATOPOEIA

Onomatopoeia is a word that actually imitates the sound as it is happening.

Examples: Slam!   Slush!
            Boom!   POW!

Below are Onomatopoeia words, illustrate them as you would see them in a comic strip, cartoon or in one of your stories.

Boom	Buzz	Bang
Click	Pop	Roar
Whoosh	Crack	Tap

ONOMATOPOEIA

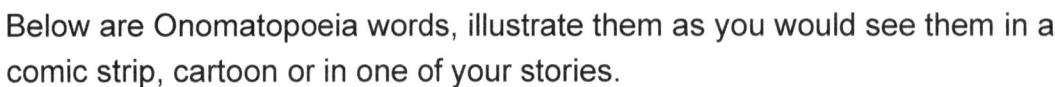

Onomatopoeia is a word that actually imitates the sound as it is happening.

Examples: Slam! Slush!
Boom! POW!

Below are Onomatopoeia words, illustrate them as you would see them in a comic strip, cartoon or in one of your stories.

Sizzle	Hiss	Cuckoo
Zip	Quack	Vroom
Beep	Achoo	Tick tock

50 R1154 ISBN: 978-1-4877-0441-4 © On The Mark Press

ONOMATOPOEIA

Read the sentence below. Match the right Onomatopoeia with the right group of words.

| click | woof | crunch | crackle | crash |
| smash | flush | ring | bang | splash |

1. the sound of burning wood _____
2. a toilet chain being pulled _____
3. the doorbell _____
4. jumping into a lake _____
5. two cars in an accident _____
6. the fire cracker _____
7. walking on little rocks _____
8. playing with a switch _____
9. the sound of broken glass _____
10. the dog barking _____

Now write five sentences using Onomatopoeia.

1. _____
2. _____
3. _____
4. _____
5. _____

OXYMORON

An oxymoron are two words together that contradict themselves.

Example: jumbo shrimp (jumbo is big but shrimp is small)

Pretty ugly (pretty & ugly – how can one be pretty and ugly?)

Bitter sweet (how can it be both bitter and sweet?)

Plastic glasses (are the glasses made out of plastic?)

Read the words below.

1. half	2. living	3. quiet	4. alone	5. home
6. upside	7. junk	8. silent	9. blind	10. second
11. beautiful	12. clearly	13. freezer	14. only	15. true

Now read the words below and match the number with its letter to form an oxymoron.

a. dead	b. tyrant	c. confused	d. burn	e. noise
f. together	g. scream	h. eye	i. best	j. full
k. work	l. down	m. food	n. story	o. choice

1 _____ 2 _____ 3 _____ 4 _____ 5 _____
6 _____ 7 _____ 8 _____ 9 _____ 10 _____
11 _____ 12 _____ 13 _____ 14 _____ 15 _____

Now write five sentences using oxymoron.

1. _____

2. _____

3. _____

4. _____

5. _____

EXPLAINING OXYMORON

Read the sentences below. Circle the oxymoron and explain each oxymoron in the sentences below.

1. She ate the larger half of the cranberry muffin.
   _____

2. Isn't there a TV show called the Living Dead?
   _____

3. My brother was proud that he was second best in math.
   _____

4. There was a major accident at the four corners yesterday, it was a minor miracle that no one was hurt.
   _____

5. My dad loves junk food.
   _____

6. Once again he bothered the dog.
   _____

7. My steak tasted like it had freezer burn.
   _____

8. The librarian told him in a loud whisper to be quiet.
   _____

9. I didn't want to turn a blind eye to the cheating going on during the exam.
   _____

10. When I mentioned the new idea we had, it went over like a lead balloon.
    _____

 R1154 ISBN: 978-1-4877-0441-4 © On The Mark Press

PUN

A pun is a joke that depends on a specific word having more than one meaning. The joke (or laughter) comes when the one listening is thinking the wrong word.

There are three types of PUNS.

Substitution Pun: This is when the listener is expecting to hear a word but a different word is chosen.

Homonym Pun: These puns sound the same but the spelling is different (tail, tale, sail, sale, steak, stake).

Double Meaning Puns: These puns use words that have more than one meaning (fair – carnival, fair – equal).

Example: What did the boss say when he sold it at the carnival? He thought it was a fair deal.

Read each sentence below. Circle the pun. Then explain the pun in your own words in the space below.

1. Helen spent her vacation sunbathing and reading novels. By the time she got back home she was well-red.

2. I offered a clown my seat on the bus because I thought it would be a nice jester.

3. We like to party with the construction workers because they really raise the roof.

4. What is the chicken farmer's favourite kind of car? A coupe.

5. I'm not much of a breakfast eater, but I do find a boiled egg first thing in the morning hard to beat.

Now write your own pun.

1. _____

2. _____

3. _____

4. _____

5. _____

54   R1154 ISBN: 978-1-4877-0441-4 © On The Mark Press

RIDDLES

Riddles are a fun way to play with words. Below are a few riddles to give you the idea. Read them and work with your classmates to figure out the answers. Once you are familiar with the riddles, try and write riddles of your own.

1. What has a single eye but can't see?

_____

2. I'm light as a feather yet even the strongest man can't hold me for more than 5 minutes. What am I?

_____

3. What goes into water black but comes out red?

_____

4. What stays where it is even when it goes off?

_____

5. You throw away the outside, eat part of the inside and then throw out the inside that is left. What am I?

_____

6. Why can't a man living in Chicago be buried in New York City?

_____

7. What do these words have in common? Madam, civic, eye, level

_____

8. How can a man go eight days without sleep?

_____

9. I am an insect. The first part of my name is also an insect. What am I?

_____

10. Which part of a boat do shopaholics like most?

_____

WORKSHEET

Use this worksheet for writing different sentences that you have learned about in this book.

_____

1. _____

_____

2. _____

_____

3. _____

_____

4. _____

_____

5. _____

_____

6. _____

_____

7. _____

_____

8. _____

_____

9. _____

_____

10. _____

TONGUE TWISTERS

A tongue twister is a sentence or a series of words which is difficult to say quickly either because of the alliteration used or similar words and sounds. Tongue twisters are sayings that are fun to play with, but have no meaning.

Example   Purple paper people purple paper people purple paper people

Betty bought some butter but the butter was bitter, so Betty bought some better butter to make the bitter butter better.

Now write your own tongue twisters. Begin with three words starting with the same letter. Write the three words three times. Practise reading them clearly and the more you practise the quicker you go.

1. _____ _____ _____. _____ _____
   _____. _____ _____ _____.

2. _____ _____ _____. _____ _____
   _____. _____ _____ _____.

3. _____ _____ _____. _____ _____
   _____. _____ _____ _____.

Now choose three words (better bitter butter) _____ _____ _____
and write a tongue twister with the three words.

1. _____
   _____

2. _____
   _____

TONGUE TWISTERS

A tongue twister is a sentence or a series of words which is difficult to say quickly either because of the alliteration used or similar words and sounds. Tongue twisters are sayings that are fun to play with, but have no meaning.

Example: I thought a thought. But the thought I thought wasn't the thought I thought I thought.

Now chose a verb and see what you can write using the example above.

1. _____

_____

2. _____

_____

Choose one of your favourite tongue twisters and illustrate it below. Share and compare tongue twisters with your classmates.

COLON

When do you use a colon? You use a colon (:) in a sentence when you are introducing a list. Using the example of camping supplies below, create various lists. The first part of the sentence (before the colon) should stand alone as a sentence. Use commas to space each item within your list.

When I go camping, I need to bring the following items: tent, sleeping bag, food and clothes.

cooler	ice	thermos	stove	fuel
matches	charcoal	silverware	potholders	pots
frying pans	tongs	shoes	boots	jeans
shorts	t-shirts	socks	hat	jacket
underwear	toothbrush	toothpaste	deodorant	comb
hairbrush	toilet	paper	tent stakes	tarps
axe	medications	bandages	antiseptic	food
gauze pads	cotton swabs	tweezers	safety pins	soap

1 (shelter)

___

2 (bedding)

___

3 (clothes)

___

4 (kitchen supplies)

___

5 (first aid)

___

6 (personal items)

___

COLON, SEMICOLON, DASH

When do you use a colon? You use a **colon** (:) in a sentence when you are introducing a list.

A **semicolon** (;) is used to separate two similar ideas in the same sentence.

A **dash** (-) can separate an idea from an afterthought.

Read the sentence below and re-write them with the appropriate punctuation.

1 Please bring with you a towel a bathing suit flip-flops and a snack.

_____

2 The game was cancelled it was raining.

_____

3 You would love it here wish you were here.

_____

4 The shopping list includes milk bread bananas and butter.

_____

5 The movie theatre was packed people have been waiting for months for this movie.

_____

6 She called me over as if I wanted to go.

_____

7 We had to stop playing supper was ready.

_____

8 I did all my homework I played outside.

_____

9 My favourite meals are lasagna, pasta, tacos, sushi and pizza.

_____

COLON, COMMA, SEMI-COLON or DASH

Good reminders – when to use which

Colon:
- Can divide yet keeps a complete sentence.
- Can divide two complete sentences.
- Can separate a theme from its list.

Comma:
- Can divide yet keeps a complete sentence.

Semi colon:
- Can divide two complete sentences.
- Can combine two clauses- the second being an afterthought.

Dash:
- Can be used to separate a comment from the rest of the sentence.

WRITING PARAGRAPHS

Is it important before we write paragraphs to understand how paragraphs are written. Paragraphs have a structure. This structure is important for you as a writer for guidance but it is also important to your reader. Therefore your paragraph needs to be clear and structured as such.

Each paragraph has:
- a main idea (could also be called subject/topic)
- a topic sentence that will introduce the topic in your paragraph
- supporting details (rule of thumb is 3 supporting details)
- concluding sentence

Main Idea: The main idea in your paragraph.

Topic Sentence: More specifically now, exactly what about your main topic will you talk about.

Supporting Sentences: 3 to 5 supporting details that are introduced by your topic sentence and then summed up with the concluding sentence.

Concluding Sentence: The concluding sentence will retell what your topic sentence was talking about, but will use other words.

MAIN IDEA

Read the paragraphs below. Write the Main Ideas on the line provided.

A hotdog is a long bread holding a sausage. The sausages can be grilled, broiled or steamed. The dressing on the hotdog can include ketchup, mustard, relish, cold slaw, tomatoes and some will add in cheese. An all American favourite, you can find hotdogs at fairs, carnivals, sports events and is an easy meal when on a picnic and/or camping.

Main Idea: _____

Yarn is a long continuous length of interlocked fibers, suitable for use in the production of many different crafts such as, textiles, sewing, crocheting, knitting, weaving embroidery and rope making. Thread is a very thin yarn to be sewn by hand or using a machine. Rope is a thicker yarn used for heavier projects such as plant holders and/or hammocks.

Main Idea: _____

The students in Ms. Deborah's class went to the sugar shack on a fieldtrip. They saw animals there such as: goats, horses, dogs, pigs, and sheep at the petting zoo. The man explained how the sap was removed from the trees, and what was done to the sap. The sap was boiled for a long time so it too, would turn into syrup. They ate bacon, eggs, potatoes, pancakes all drowned in syrup.

Main Idea: _____

MAIN IDEA

Read the paragraphs below. Write the Main Ideas on the line provided.

One should try to go for a walk regularly. Walking will get you to get light exercise. It will help you to breathe in the fresh air. It will help your senses as you smell the flowers, hear the birds, and see your surroundings. Walking helps you to digest your meal after it is eaten. If you walk before your meal, you will appreciate it more once you get home.

Main Idea: _____

It is important to show good sportsmanship when playing any game or sport. It is important to play fair. One should play honestly and respect the rules, the other players, and the referees. It is also important to be cheerful even if you have lost. It's all in playing the game rather than winning all the games.

Main Idea: _____

Flowers are beautiful. They are part of the beauty of nature. Many flowers are associated with specific events. The red rose is often a symbol of love for weddings or Valentine's Day. Flowers come in many colours. They have been around for thousands of years.

Main Idea: _____

MAIN IDEA

Read the paragraphs below. Write the Main Ideas on the line provided.

You can make perfectly great toast for breakfast in these easy steps. First, take two slices of bread and put them in the toaster and press the button. Then take out butter and jam from the fridge. Take out a butter knife from the drawer and a plate from the cabinet. Then pour yourself a glass of milk. Next, you wait till the toaster dings to tell you the toast is ready. Place the toast on the plate and spread the butter and jam using the butter knife. Now you are ready to eat your toast.

Main Idea: _____

There are many interesting facts on owls. First, most owls are nocturnal which means they hunt at night and sleep during the day. Next, owls are not able to move their eyes within the socket therefore they must move their head from side to side to see. Finally, the smallest owl is called the Elf owl and he stands no more than 6 inches long and he has a wingspan of 15 inches wide. Owls are very fascinating birds.

Main Idea: _____

It is very important to know how to write paragraphs. It is the base of the written language. Everyone should know how to write a paragraph as writing and reading go hand in hand. There is structure to writing a paragraph. This structure helps your reader with the message that you want to convey. In writing good paragraphs, a writer can communicate his/her thoughts better.

Main Idea: _____

WRITING TOPIC SENTENCES

Read the details below and write a Topic Sentence for each.

Going to a Baseball Game:

- find out when and where the game is
- get tickets
- get money
- what is the weather like
- what time is the game at

Topic Sentence: _____.

Bicycle:

- get to and from school
- need to lock
- exercise
- get home sooner (no bus or no daycare)
- regular maintenance

Topic Sentence: _____.

Pets:

- unconditional love
- companion
- teaches responsibilities
- something to love and cuddle
- daily exercise

Topic Sentence: _____.

WRITING TOPIC SENTENCES

Read the details below and write a Topic Sentence for each.

Homemade Playdough:

- get recipe
- get ingredients (flour, salt, water, food colouring)
- what items you need (bowl, spoon, rolling pin)
- set area
- get playdough and cookie cutters and create

Topic Sentence: _____.

Dr. Seuss:

- real name Theodor Seuss Geisel
- pen name Theo LeSieg, Rosetta Stone, Theophrastus Seuss
- served as the commander of the Animation Department of the First Motion Picture Unit of the United States Army Air Forces in World War II
- 1st book, And to Think That I Saw It on Mulberry Street, was rejected by publishers 27 times
- has won at least: two Academy awards, two Emmy awards, a Peabody award, the Laura Ingalls Wilder Medal, and the Pulitzer Prize.

Topic Sentence: _____.

Turkeys:

- male turkeys are called "gobblers"
- after the "gobble" call they make to announce themselves to females
- females turkeys are called "hens"
- other turkey sounds include "purrs," "yelps" and "kee-kees."
- an adult gobbler weighs 16 to 22 pounds on average

Topic Sentence: _____.

WRITING TOPIC SENTENCES

Add details in the box and write the Topic Sentence for each box on the line.

Topic Sentence: _____.

Topic Sentence: _____.

Topic Sentence: _____.

WRITING SUPPORTING DETAILS

Read the Topic Sentences below. Add 3-5 supporting details based on the Topic Sentence.

1. Reading is the most important subject in school because you need to be able to read to learn all the other subjects.

   _____

   _____

   _____

   _____

   _____

2. It is important to be a good person to others and to yourself.

   _____

   _____

   _____

   _____

   _____

WRITING SUPPORT SENTENCES

Read the Topic Sentences below. Add 3-5 supporting details based on the Topic Sentence.

3. It is important for school subjects such as Art, Music and Drama to come back into the curriculum because they have a lot to offer.

_____

_____

_____

_____

_____

4. Fieldtrips are an important part of the school curriculum and should be where students don't always have a chance to go.

_____

_____

_____

_____

_____

WRITING SUPPORT SENTENCES

Read the Topic Sentences below. Add 3-5 supporting details based on the Topic Sentence.

5. I would love to be able to play the piano because I love the music coming from that instrument.

_____

_____

_____

_____

_____

6. Swimming classes should be part of the school curriculum for all students.

_____

_____

_____

_____

_____

CONCLUDING SENTENCE

The Concluding Sentence of a paragraph is the last sentence of the paragraph. It basically retells the reader what the topic was using different words. It will sum up the paragraph.

Read each Topic Sentence below and write your own Concluding Sentence.

1. TOPIC SENTENCE: If you don't sleep well at night, your health will suffer.

   CONCLUDING SENTENCE: _____

   _____

2. TOPIC SENTENCE: Bees work together for the good of their queen and their hive.

   CONCLUDING SENTENCE: _____

   _____

3. TOPIC SENTENCE: Summer is a great time to focus on exercising outdoors.

   CONCLUDING SENTENCE: _____

   _____

4. TOPIC SENTENCE: You can learn a lot from talking with your grandparents.

   CONCLUDING SENTENCE: _____

   _____

5. TOPIC SENTENCE: The more you study, the more you will learn.

   CONCLUDING SENTENCE: _____

   _____

CONCLUDING SENTENCE

The Concluding Sentence of a paragraph is the last sentence and sums up the paragraph. Now use the Topic Sentences and write a Concluding Sentence.

1 TOPIC SENTENCE: Reading is the most important subject in school because you need to be able to read to learn all the other subjects.

CONCLUDING SENTENCE: _____

_____

2 TOPIC SENTENCE: It is important to be a good person to others and to yourself.

CONCLUDING SENTENCE: _____

_____

3 TOPIC SENTENCE: It is important for school subjects such as Art, Music and Drama to come back into the curriculum because they have a lot to offer.

CONCLUDING SENTENCE: _____

_____

4 TOPIC SENTENCE: Fieldtrips are an important part of the school curriculum and should be where students don't always have a chance to go.

CONCLUDING SENTENCE: _____

_____

5 TOPIC SENTENCE: I would love to be able to play the piano because I love the music coming from that instrument.

CONCLUDING SENTENCE: _____

_____

6 TOPIC SENTENCE: Swimming classes should be part of the school curriculum for all students.

CONCLUDING SENTENCE: _____

_____

Now that you have added the Concluding Sentence, go back and get the supporting details you added on pages to 69, 70 and 71 and write the paragraphs using the worksheet on page 74.

PARAGRAPH WORKSHEET

TOPIC SENTENCE: _____

_____

Supporting idea #1 _____

_____

_____

Supporting idea #2 _____

_____

_____

Supporting idea #3 _____

_____

_____

CONCLUSION: _____

_____

_____

4 TYPES OF WRITING

DESCRIPTIVE WRITING IDEAS

Descriptive writing says exactly as it is called DESCRIPTIVE. The object or subject is described in full details. You want your reader to be able to see what you see– therefore details, colours, lighting etc. are all important.

NARRATIVE WRITING IDEAS

Narrative Writing is the term used when a writer writes similar to when you write a paragraph: a central point, specific supporting details and they are written in a clearly structured and organized manner.

EXPOSITORY WRITING IDEAS

Expository Writing is the term used when a writer writes a message that conveys information and explains ideas. It can explain, describe, define, instruct and inform. It will be factual. It is not like Persuasive or creative writing. It is a how-to, step-by-step, instructional piece. This piece will include clear, logical transitions and the paragraphs will support the information given.

PERSUASIVE/ARGUMENTATIVE SENTENCE STARTERS

Persuasive writing is the term used when a writer writes to influence someone or something. Taking a stand or expressing an opinion, giving supporting details that support your opinion or argument or opinion could result in having people change their minds. If your writing isn't clear, and the supporting details aren't strong, changing someone or something will not happen.

DESCRIPTIVE WRITING IDEAS

Descriptive writing is exactly as it is called DESCRIPTIVE. The object or subject is described in full details. You want your reader to be able to see what you see – therefore details, colours, lighting etc. are all important.

1. a bowl of fruit
2. a cell phone
3. a character from a book, movie, or television program
4. a Christmas tree
5. a city bus or subway train
6. a favourite restaurant
7. a Halloween costume
8. a hospital emergency room
9. a laptop computer
10. a painting
11. a photograph
12. a refrigerator or washing machine
13. a rest room in a service station a secret hiding place
14. a small town cemetery
15. a storefront window
16. a street that leads to your home or school
17. a treasured belonging
18. a vase of flowers
19. a waiting room
20. a work table

DESCRIPTIVE WRITING IDEAS

21. an accident scene
22. an art exhibit
23. an ideal apartment
24. an inspiring view
25. an item left too long in your refrigerator
26. an unusual room
27. backstage during a play or a concert
28. the inside of a car
29. the scene at a concert or athletic event
30. your closet
31. your dream room
32. your father
33. your favourite food
34. your ideal classmate
35. your locker
36. your memory of a place that you visited
37. your mother
38. your pet

Brainstorm and add more writing prompts to your list.

_____

_____

_____

NARRATIVE WRITING IDEAS

Narrative Writing is the term used when a writer writes similar to when you write a paragraph: a central point, specific supporting details and they are written in a clearly structured and organized manner. Below are many writing prompts.

1. a memorable family event
2. an exciting minute or two of a soccer game (or other sporting event)
3. a memorable moment of failure or success
4. an encounter that changed your life
5. first day at a new class or school
6. an experience that left you disillusioned
7. an embarrassing experience
8. a frightening experience
9. a memorable journey
10. your first visit to the countryside (or to a large city)
11. the circumstances that led to the breakup of a friendship
12. a brush with greatness
13. a brush with death
14. a time that you took a stand on an important issue
15. an experience that altered your view of someone

NARRATIVE WRITING IDEAS

16. a trip that you would like to take

17. a vacation trip

18. an account of a visit to a fictional place

19. your first time away from home

20. traffic accident

Brainstorm ideas with some classmates and add more writing prompts.

_____

_____

_____

_____

_____

_____

_____

_____

_____

_____

_____

EXPOSITORY WRITING IDEAS

Expository Writing is the term used when a writer writes a message that conveys information and explains ideas. It can explain, describe, define, instruct and inform. It will be factual. It is not like Persuasive or creative writing. It is a how-to, step-by-step, instructional piece. This piece will include clear, logical transitions and the paragraphs will support the information given.

Below are different Expository ideas:

1. Many students are worried about succeeding in school. Create a piece of writing that you could turn into a flyer for students and their parents on the subject on Being a Successful Student.

2. The world is a huge place and unfortunately we can't visit everywhere. Choose a location that you would like to visit. Create a piece of writing that you could turn into a travel brochure on the location you have chosen. Mention important facts such as foods eaten there, music, leisure activities, schooling, culture and/or religion, main attractions.

3. What is the best invention to date? Why has this invention been helpful to others? How could you, as an inventor improve that invention? Write a paper that explains why and how.

4. Think of the most valuable handmade item. Write a piece about it, how it was made, by whom, its use and why you cherish this handmade item.

5. Ancestry look ups are very interesting to many people. Write a paper on your last name. Where are the origins? What information can you share about your name? What information has left you asking for more?

6. Do you remember in Kindergarten, the teacher made us participate in Show & Tell? It was important socially to be able to talk about something important to us, it made us practise our public speaking and helped us to make bonds with our fellow classmates. Write about an item that you would bring for Show & Tell, now in your present class. What would your item be? Why?

7. If you could improve something in your school as of right now, what would that change be? How would you go about making that change? How would you get the teachers and principal on board? Would parents agree to the change?

8. Think of your favourite pet. Write a piece about your favourite pet. What pet was it? Name? Information about this pet, why was this pet so special to you?

9. We are all Life Long Learners. We learn both in and out of school. Write a piece telling about something that you have learned recently. Where do you learn this? How did you confirm that in fact you just learned it? Have you shared it with anyone?

EXPOSITORY WRITING IDEAS

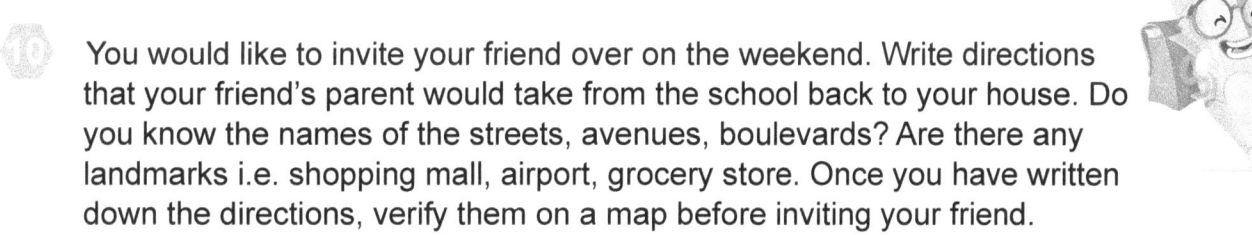

10. You would like to invite your friend over on the weekend. Write directions that your friend's parent would take from the school back to your house. Do you know the names of the streets, avenues, boulevards? Are there any landmarks i.e. shopping mall, airport, grocery store. Once you have written down the directions, verify them on a map before inviting your friend.

11. Next Monday, a new student will be arriving in your class. Write a piece of introduction to this new student. What procedure should this student know of from day one?

12. Each child has a special place within its family. First born, middle child, last born, only child. Write a piece that shares your position within your family. What are the advantages and disadvantages to being in that position?

13. We all have a special corner to hide in our house. Write about where you like to hide. Where is it located? Does everyone in your family know? When do you use this special corner?

14. You would like the principal in your school to change the cafeteria menu. Write a piece explaining the necessary changes that need to be done. What new menu would you like to propose?

15. We all have a special family member. Write about your special family member. Who is this person? Why are they so special to you? What special things have you or will you do together?

16. Every community and culture have something special they share. Write a piece about a specific culture and what do they share that is special and unique to them Remember that you are writing this for someone who does not share that community and/or culture. What are the important characteristics that need to be known?

17. Many of us love music. What is your favourite type of music? How did you discover this music? Who do you share this music with? Who are one of the top artists in this type of music?

18. We all love fieldtrips. What was the best fieldtrip you EVER went on? Where did you go? When did you go? Who went with you? Why is this fieldtrip so important and/or memorable?

19. One of your fellow classmates is having difficulty with a math concept. You, on the other hand are doing quite well with that concept. Write a piece that would inform your friend about the math concept. Would specific instructions be helpful? Would the students clearly understand what you are trying to get them to understand?

20. You have one favourite dish but you can't find the recipe to share with your classmates at school. Write the recipe, the ingredients, presentation and any other important details your friends will need to make this recipe at home.

PERSUASIVE/ARGUMENTATIVE SENTENCE STARTERS

Persuasive writing is the term used when a writer writes to influence someone or something. Taking a stand or expressing an opinion, giving supporting details that support your opinion or argument or opinion could result in having people change their minds. If your writing isn't clear, and the supporting details aren't strong, changing someone or something will not happen. Below you will find persuasive sentence starters to practise writing persuasive arguments.

- In my opinion…
- In my point-of-view…
- I honestly believe…
- I have to say that…
- I know that…
- I'm sure that…
- It is clear to me that…
- I am absolutely certain…
- The time has come to …
- It seems to me that…
- Furthermore…
- Although, I agree…
- In addition to…
- Without a doubt…
- According to _____ …
- Some people have expressed…
- Obviously…

Can you add more persuasive sentence starters?

_____   _____

_____   _____

_____   _____

ANSWER KEY

1,3,4,5,6,8,9,10 -yes #2

1. ran, is running, will run 2. jumped, is jumping, will jump
3. skipped, is skipping, will skip 4. laughed, is laughing, will laugh
5. leaped. is leaping, will leap 6. shot, is shooting, will shoot
7. dribbled, is dribbling, will dribble 8. passed, is passing, will pass
9. sat, is sitting, will sit 10. printed, is sprinting, will sprint
11. blocked, is blocking, will block 12. ate, is eating, will eat
13. wrote, is writing, will write 14. slept, is sleeping, will sleep
15. walked, is walking, will walk

1. present 2. past 3. present 4. present 5. future 6. present 7. passed 8. past
9. Future 10. present

1. sang 2. were 3. went 4. had 5. read 6. paid 7. all 3 8. know, knew 9. stood
10. rang 11. forgot 12. drank 13. grew, grow 14. froze 15. lost 16. hid 17. bit
18. became 19. got 20. began

1. alliteration 2. hyperbole 3. similes 4. metaphor 5. personification 6. hyperbole
7. alliteration 8. alliteration 9. similes 10. hyperbole 11. similes 12. metaphor
13. similes 14. personification 15. metaphor

1.onomatopoeia 2. idiom 3. oxymoron 4. pun 5. understatement 6. oxymoron
7. oxymoron 8. idiom 9 idiom 10. onomatopoeia 11.pun 12. onomatopoeia
13. idioms 14. oxymoron 15. understatement.

1.b 2.c 3.b 4.c 5.b 6.a

Matching: 1.b 2.c 3.d 4.a 5.f 6.e
Rewriting: 1.d, 2.e, 3.c, 4.a, 5.f, 6.b

ANSWER KEY

Page 47: 1.c 2.c 3.c 4.b 5.b 6.c

Page 48: Matching: 1.b 2.d 3 a or e 4.a or e 5.h 6.g 7.e 8.c Answers will vary.

Page 51: 1. crackle 2. flush 3. ring 4. splash 5. crash 6. bang 7. crunch 8. click
9. smash 10. woof

Page 52: 1.half full 2.living dead 3.quiet scream or quiet noise 4.alone together
5.home work 6.upside down 7.junk food 8.silent noise or silent scream 9. blind eye
10. second best 11. beautiful tyrant 12. clearly confused 13. freezer burn
14. only choice 15. true story

Answers may vary for the following pages: 10, 11, 12, 13, 14, 15, 16, 17, 18, 19, 23, 24, 25, 26, 27, 28, 29, 32, 33, 34, 35, 36, 37, 55, 56, 57, 58 59, 60, 61, 64, 65, 66, 67, 68, 69, 70, 71, 72 73, 74, 75, 85

CHEAT SHEET

Just like in math and science, creating your own Cheat Sheet of useful information, in your own words is priceless. In this book we covered many types of sentences, questions, figures of speech. Use the chart below to add in your own definition and/or example.

www.ingramcontent.com/pod-product-compliance
Lightning Source LLC
Chambersburg PA
CBHW080349170426
43194CB00014B/2733